Summer Green to Autumn Gold

To Raul

Thank you to Dr. Dana A. Dudle, Winona H. Welch Professor of Biology at DePauw University, for reviewing the text and illustrations for accuracy

Millbrook Press™
An imprint of Lerner Publishing Group, Inc.
241 First Avenue North
Minneapolis, MN 55401 USA

For reading levels and more information, look up this title at www.lernerbooks.com.

Designed by Emily Harris.
Main body text set in HandySans.
Typeface provided by MADType.
The illustrations in this book were created using cut paper collage with watercolor.

Library of Congress Cataloging-in-Publication Data

Names: Posada, Mia, author, illustrator.
Title: Summer green to autumn gold : uncovering leaves' hidden colors / by Mia Posada.
Description: Minneapolis : Millbrook Press, [2020] | Audience: Age 5–10. | Audience: K to Grade 3.
Identifiers: LCCN 2018047652 (print) | LCCN 2018048344 (ebook) | ISBN 9781541560994 (eb pdf) | ISBN 9781541528994 (lb : alk. paper)
Subjects: LCSH: Leaves—Color—Juvenile literature. | Fall foliage—Juvenile literature.
Classification: LCC QK649 (ebook) | LCC QK649 .P67 2020 (print) | DDC 581.4/8—dc23

LC record available at https://lccn.loc.gov/2018047652

Manufactured in the United States of America
4-1009351-35703-3/20/2023

SUMMER GREEN TO AUTUMN GOLD

UNCOVERING LEAVES' HIDDEN COLORS

MIA POSADA

Millbrook Press/Minneapolis

red maple

honey locust

What kinds of leaves do you see in the summer?

aspen

linden

willow

ginko

bur oak

sugar maple

paper birch

silver maple

white oak

black walnut

sweet gum

dogwood

elm

cottonwood

ash

From **emerald** to **jade** and every shade in between, summer leaves fill the world with **green**!

The secret to their **green** color is found deep inside each leaf.

Tiny parts in the leaf called cells hold even tinier parts called chloroplasts. And inside the chloroplasts is something called chlorophyll.

Chlorophyll is a green pigment, or color.

It is what makes leaves green.

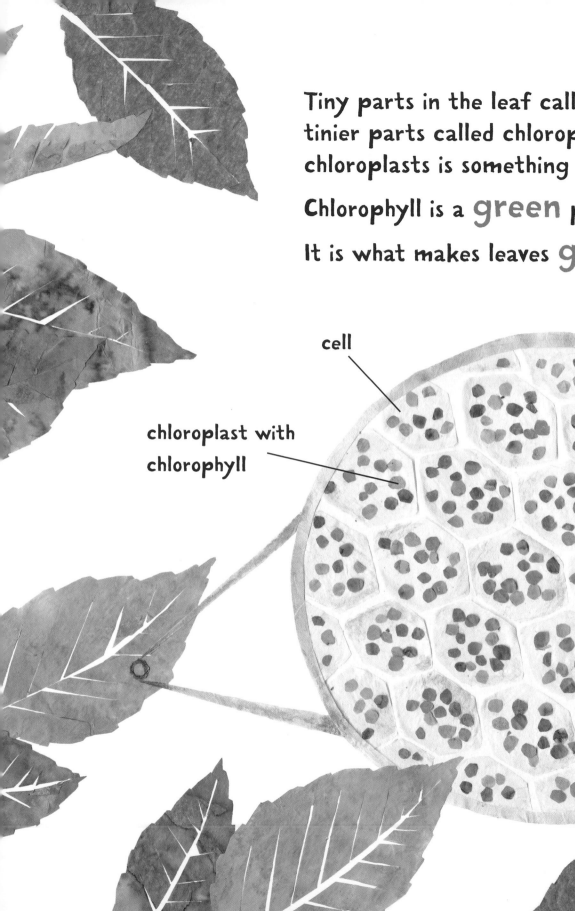

cell

chloroplast with chlorophyll

Besides making plants green, chlorophyll has a job to do. It helps make food for trees and other green plants.

When the sun **shines** on a plant's leaves, chlorophyll collects some of its energy. The energy combines with water from the ground and gas from the air to make food. The food helps the plant **grow**.

The green chlorophyll is also hiding something.

It is covering up other colors inside the leaf. Orange and yellow pigments hide beneath the bright green.

All through the warm summer, they wait.

Slowly, summer **creeps** toward fall.

The air **cools**, and the nights grow longer.

These changes tell trees it is time to get ready for winter.

The growing season for trees is over. The leaves stop making food. They don't need chlorophyll anymore.

The chlorophyll slowly disappears, and the leaves' green color fades away.

Now the hidden yellows and oranges are finally revealed!

Some leaves turn **fiery red**, **deep purple**, or **bright pink**. These bright colors form inside the leaf as the weather cools.

Other leaves have brown pigments hidden inside. **As** the chlorophyll fades, these leaves turn **brown**.

Many leaves have mixtures of yellow, orange, red, and brown pigments.

The world is a rainbow of scarlet and orange, burgundy and gold.

Soon the stems of the leaves start to separate from the tree. The wind **blows** them loose.

They **drift** to the ground. **Piling** up.

The fallen leaves **feed** the forest floor. They break down and become part of the soil.

They become food and shelter for insects, snails, and worms.

The bare trees **sleep**
through the winter.

This is their **resting** time.

In spring, fresh leaves sprout from awakening buds, full of chlorophyll and filling the world with **green** again!

DIFFERENT KINDS OF LEAVES

The trees in this book whose leaves change color and fall off every year are called deciduous trees. Their leaves are soft and too fragile to survive a freezing winter. The stems of the leaves seal off to protect the tree from drying out and from infection. In doing so, the leaves are released.

Some trees, called evergreens, keep most of their leaves all year long. Evergreens such as pine and spruce trees have hardy needlelike leaves with a protective waxy coating that helps them survive the cold of winter.

PIGMENTS IN NATURE

The pigments that give leaves their vibrant orange and yellow fall colors are called carotenoids. Carotenoids are found all over the plant world. They are what make carrots and pumpkins orange, and bananas, corn, and daffodils bright yellow.

Red and purple leaf colors are made by anthocyanin pigments. Anthocyanins also make apples red and form the reds, pinks, purples, and blues of flower petals.

Brown colors in leaves are made by tannins. In early fall, the tannins interact with the carotenoid and anthocyanin pigments to create the golds, burgundies, and rich coppers in leaves such as oaks. Later in fall, the orange, yellow, and red pigments fade out of the leaves, leaving only the brown tannins.

Some or all of these pigments may be present in a single leaf. They combine and interact to form the vibrant spectrum of fall colors.

FALL COLORS AROUND THE WORLD

Fall leaves are most vibrant in regions of the world that have four distinct seasons. In areas where the weather doesn't turn cold, leaves may fall but usually do not change color.

The types of trees in an area determine the color and intensity of its fall leaves. For instance, the forests of the Northeast United States contain many maple trees that produce vibrant reds. The aspen trees of the Rocky Mountains produce mainly bright yellows.

FROM FALL TO FALL, COLORS CAN CHANGE

The colors and brilliance of the leaves on a particular tree may vary from year to year. The brightness of the pigments can be affected by the weather. Autumn weather with lots of bright sunny days and cool nights will produce the brightest fall leaves. The red and purple anthocyanin pigments need sunlight in order to form, so a cloudy fall will not produce as many bright reds. A very dry summer may delay the leaves' turning or they may fall before they have a chance to turn. Freezing fall temperatures will destroy the leaves' ability to form red and purple anthocyanin pigments. The factors that affect leaf colors can create different colors even on the same tree. The side of a tree that gets the most sunlight will have the brightest red leaves.

Glossary

anthocyanins (an-thuh-SY-uh-nihnz): pigments that give leaves red or purple colors

carotenoids (kuh-RA-tuh-noydz): pigments that give leaves yellow or orange colors

cell: the basic unit of any living thing

chlorophyll (KLOHR-uh-fihl): a pigment inside chloroplasts, which are inside plant cells, that makes leaves green and helps make food for plants

chloroplasts (KLOHR-uh-plast): small parts inside plant cells that contain chlorophyll

deciduous (dih-SIHD-juh-wuhs): trees or other plants that lose their leaves every year

evergreen: a tree or other plant with leaves that remain green all year

gas: a substance, such as air, that spreads to fill any space that holds it. Leaves take in a gas called carbon dioxide from the air to make food for plants.

pigments (PIG-muhntz): substances that give color to animals and plants

tannins (TA-nuhnz): substances that give leaves a brown color

Hands-on Experiments with Leaves and Pigments

Do you want to do more with leaves than collect them? Here are a few fun ideas you can try! Safety note: Be sure to ask an adult for help with these experiments.

Coffee Filter Experiment
http://www.sciencefun.org/kidszone/experiments/changing-of-the-leaves/

Leaf Pigment Extraction
http://alittlepinchofperfect.com/fall-leaf-science-experiment-for-kids/

Red Cabbage Anthocyanin Experiment
http://www.easy-science-experiments.com/anthocyanin.html